Original title:
Candy Canes and Christmas Dreams

Author: Micah Sterling
ISBN HARDBACK: 978-9916-90-880-8
ISBN PAPERBACK: 978-9916-90-881-5

Festive Colors in Brisk Breezes

Stripes of red in frosty air,
Laughter bounces everywhere.
Jingle bells on wildly spun,
Slip on ice and call it fun!

Shiny bows on neighbor's hats,
Chasing squirrels and playful chats.
Snowflakes dance like tiny clowns,
Painting smiles on winter towns.

Novelty Treats Beneath the Tree

Gummy bears with funny faces,
Hiding in the strangest places.
Lollipops and jellybeans,
Join the crazy candy scenes.

Funky socks with polka dots,
Chocolate bars with silly thoughts.
Fruitcake jokes that never land,
Wrapped in ribbons left unplanned.

Frosty Paths and Holiday Echoes

Hopping high on icicle rails,
Mapping out our merry trails.
Giggles burst like bubbles fine,
Sliding down the perfect line.

Chill and thrill in every cheer,
Frosty whispers loud and clear.
Echoes dance in frosty air,
Joyful shouts beyond compare.

Lanterns of Cheer in the Silent Night

Glow-in-the-dark with silly grins,
Bouncing lights like playful pins.
Guide the way with bubbles bright,
Twinkling stars in grateful flight.

Laughter shared by the glowing flame,
Every shadow knows our name.
In the stillness, magic thrives,
Whispered tales and jolly jives.

Tinsel and Taffy under the Moonlight

Under the moon, the taffy glows,
Twinkling bright, like a friend in rows.
Elves in the night, with hats too small,
Munching on treats, they start to sprawl.

A squirrel in a scarf, so bold, so spry,
Dancing with joy, oh me, oh my!
He snags a lollipop, oh what a sight,
Chasing his dreams under stars so bright.

Festive Notes of Delightful Flavor

In the air, a melody sweet,
Overflowing bowls with a delightful treat.
Gingerbread men doing a jig,
Frosting a hat, oh, look at him dig!

Dancing in circles, they laugh like mad,
While a cat in a cape looks terribly glad.
Each nibble and giggle, a festive spree,
Who knew sugar could spark such glee?

Luminous Treats Beneath the Mistletoe

Beneath the mistletoe, the lights do shine,
With jelly beans rolling in a crooked line.
A reindeer prances, just lost his way,
Chasing his friends in a candy bouquet.

Marshmallow clouds float high in the air,
Snowmen conspiring with a marshmallow glare.
Twinkling and giggling, they share a kiss,
A peppermint swirled in sweet, sugary bliss.

Scrumptious Hopes on a Silent Evening

On a night so still, with giggles so loud,
Chocolates are dancing, attracting a crowd.
With sprinkles and laughter, they twirl and spin,
A sugar-coated world, where fun can begin.

Oh, cupcakes complain that they're losing their fluff,
As frosting gets wild, and the whipped cream gets tough.
A joyous parade of flavors so bright,
In a whimsical land of delightfully light.

Joyful Journeys Through Sugar's Realm

In a land where the sweet treats grow,
A gumdrop forest all aglow.
Marshmallow mountains, fluffy and bright,
We slide down on licorice, what a sight!

Frolicking fairies with jelly-bean wings,
Sprinkling laughter as each one sings.
Chocolate rivers, not too deep,
A frosty adventure, but no time for sleep!

Sugar trains on waffle tracks,
Caramel crews with sweet little hacks.
Chasing frost-flavored penguins around,
In this wild world, giggles abound!

Oh, a taffy swirl under peppermint skies,
Giggling gnomes with big gooey pies.
With each turn, more surprises unfold,
In this land of laughter, where joy is sold!

Merry Morsels in a Wonderland of Frost

In a village built of gingerbread hues,
A snowman wears gumdrops as shoes.
Fudge fountains bubble, giving a cheer,
While the cookie elves dance, spreading good cheer.

Cotton candy clouds fluffing the air,
With chocolate chip snowflakes landing with care.
Marzipan animals frolic about,
As fruity delights cause giggles to sprout.

There's a pie-eating contest, oh what a sight,
With whipped cream mustaches, it's pure delight.
Ginger snaps sprint and giggles ensue,
In this frosty wonderland, happiness grew!

A s'mores campfire under tinsel trees,
Hot cocoa rivers, a warm winter breeze.
Each bite is a giggle, a tickle of fun,
In a sugary paradise, we play till we're done!

Winter's Bounty and Sugary Bliss

Pinecone pies on a frosty plate,
Peppermint puddles, it's quite the fate.
Bouncing berries with cherries so sweet,
The dance of the desserts, a festive treat!

Wandering through marshmallow streets,
Each house sprinkled with sugary beats.
Snowflake sprinkles as big as the moon,
Join in the fun, we'll sing a sweet tune!

Silly snowflakes doing a jig,
With popsicle sticks, we all dance big.
A confetti explosion of sweet little bites,
In this winter wonderland, pure delight ignites!

So raise your glass of fizzy delight,
To a season of laughter, all merry and bright.
With sugar on our lips and joy in the air,
Let's celebrate winter with flavors to share!

Marshmallow Clouds and Evergreen Hues

In a winter land where sweets abound,
Marshmallows float, thick and round.
Trees wear ornaments, gleeful and bright,
Sipping hot cocoa, what a delight!

Snowflakes dance with a jolly cheer,
Laughter echoes, pulling us near.
Gumdrops line paths, a sugary scheme,
We stroll together, lost in the dream.

Lullabies of Light in a Savory Wonderland

Twinkling bulbs hung over the streets,
Sugarplum fairies tap little feet.
Gingerbread houses stand firm and proud,
Smiles grow wider in the festive crowd.

A chorus of giggles fills up the air,
While frosting snowmen cause a big scare.
Spoonfuls of joy drip onto our plates,
In this flavorful land, happiness waits.

Enchanted Nights with Flavors Bright

As the moon tosses sprinkles of glee,
We barter our dreams for a taste of the sea.
Chocolate rivers run deep in our hearts,
Where laughter and sweetness never depart.

Whipped cream clouds float in skies of delight,
While dance parties commence under starlight.
We spin round and round, a confection parade,
In a whimsical world where fun’s never spayed.

Starlit Wishes Wrapped in Tinsel

Night brings a glow, twinkling so grand,
A wish on the stars, playful, unplanned.
Ribboned delights, with a wink and a grin,
Each giggle and snicker draws more fun in.

Chocolate fountains splash joy everywhere,
With sprinkles that twirl in the cool winter air.
Friends gather close, with stories to share,
In this jolly realm, we shed every care.

Candied Whispers of an Evening Glow

In the corner, a treat takes a spin,
With a twist and a curl, it beckons us in.
Pink stripes like laughter, they dance on the light,
While giddy kids giggle at hints of a bite.

Sparkling shadows with sugar-coated cheer,
Tell tales of a day wrapped in warmth, oh dear!
We nibble and chuckle, the fun never wanes,
As sweet little secrets dissolve like refrains.

Luminous Confections and Cherished Songs

Under bright lights, the goodies all gleam,
With flavors quite quirky, they spark every dream.
Minty surprises that tingle the tongue,
Make voices all jolly and laughter quite young.

A chorus of flavors in a riotous mix,
As sticky delights play their whimsical tricks.
Each taste a chorus, a melody sweet,
With giggles and grins, we gather to eat.

Euphoria in Every Sweet Savor

Lollipop laughter on a snowy old street,
As frosty delights make us bounce on our feet.
The sugary wonders both fizzy and bright,
Can turn any frown into sheer pure delight.

In wrappers of joy, every flavor will sing,
With goodies like rabbits that hop in a fling.
The giggling echoes through the crisp winter air,
Each morsel a reminder that fun's everywhere.

Ethereal Dreams of Yule's Embrace

Whirl and twirl in a sugary dance,
With flavors that sweep you into a trance.
Jingles and jests in a colorful spree,
While hearts stay as warm as a cozy cup of tea.

With playful concoctions, we giggle and share,
As our hopes and our wishes float high in the air.
A banquet of joy, where whims come to play,
In the happiest moments, we cheerfully stay.

Frosted Wishes on Merry Nights

In a world of twirls and bright delight,
Silly socks dance under moonlight.
Gingerbread folks with frosting hats,
Chasing after jolly, giggling cats.

Marshmallow clouds, fluffy and round,
Elves have secrets that bubble and sound.
Whipped cream rivers that flow with glee,
Frosted wishes, oh, come sip with me!

Reindeer prance on rooftops slick,
Telling tales with a sparkle and trick.
Laughter echoes, sweet as a tune,
Nighttime whispers, let's fly to the moon!

Sweet Serenades of Holiday Cheer

Jingle bells ring with a quirky twist,
Singing carols while shaking a fist.
Mittens lost and noses red,
Slipping on ice, we giggle instead.

Hot cocoa rivers, oh what a treat,
Marshmallows launching, can't stay in your seat!
Dancing ornaments shimmy and sway,
Come join the fun, let’s laugh all day!

Pine trees whisper with a wink so sly,
Squirrels offering nuts as they pass by.
Twinkling stars wink down to cheer,
Join the parade, the season's here!

Twinkling Lights and Sugary Sights

Lights twinkle bright, playing hide and seek,
Lollipops stare with a cheeky peek.
Gumdrops invite us to take a spin,
A sugary race that's sure to win!

Fuzzy hats wobble on heads askew,
Hot pie flings and the snowman too.
Silly snowball fights, aim for the vest,
Taste the joy; this season's the best!

Candy canons, ready for blast,
Confetti sprinkles, oh, what a cast!
Bring on the giggles, don't let them fade,
In this sweet zing, we've got it made!

Crystalline Confections of Joy

Icicles hang like jewels aglow,
Sugar plums dance in a soft, sweet flow.
Crisp winter air full of giggling noise,
Wrapped up snug, we're all girls and boys!

Chiming bells ring with mischievous cheer,
Elves spinning tales that we all want to hear.
Snickerdoodles stacked high, ready to share,
Frosted delights, oh, how we dare!

Sprinkled wishes shoot up like stars,
Chocolate rivers flowing so far.
In this wonderland, joy comes alive,
With every moment, we happily thrive!

A Tapestry of Twilight and Treats

In a world where fog meets cheer,
Gingersnap elves hoot with beer.
Marshmallow snowflakes dance on high,
While sugar plums giggle and fly.

Whipped cream mountains, frosting streams,
Frostbite dreams burst at the seams.
Toffee trees with laughter sway,
As licorice monkeys lead the play.

A pudding pond with jellyfish,
Strawberry wishes in every swish.
Nutty squirrels toss candy with glee,
As taffy clouds float above the spree.

But beware the gumdrop sneeze,
Overflowing joy that's sure to tease.
In this land of sweet delight,
Every giggle lasts all night.

Frosted Whimsy and Sparkling Dreams

A peppermint bunny hops real fast,
Leaving trails of treats that never last.
Chocolate rivers flow with a grin,
While candy corn fish jump right in.

Tinsel trees with mystery wraps,
All the children take their naps.
Pudding pop stars sing so loud,
Making joy in every crowd.

Cookie clouds drift lazily by,
As caramel kisses claim the sky.
Marzipan fairies twirl and spin,
Painting laughter on every skin.

Pumpkin-heads roll off their seats,
Trying to catch the candy beats.
A giggle here, a snort or two,
Sprinkling joy like morning dew.

Scenes of Sweetness in Winter's Glow

A frosty fog of licorice mist,
Where cupcakes make the golden list.
Fudge fountains gurgle joy so sweet,
As gumdrop geese waddle on their feet.

Pudding pipes with marshmallow tunes,
Silly haikus made by raccoon raccoons.
Wobbling snowmen in jelly delight,
While brownies cheer for a snowball fight.

Lollipop owls hoot all night long,
With a wink and a jig, they hum their song.
Naughty kittens ride on candy sleighs,
Stealing treats in the cheeriest ways.

Truffle trains zoom down the tracks,
Leaving trails of chocolate snacks.
In this funny, whimsical scene,
Where every bite is fit for a queen.

Sugar-Dusted Memories Under Moonlight

Under a moon with a sugary grin,
Fruity lollipops spin and spin.
Cinnamon bears in a friendly race,
Smiling wide with a sprinkle of grace.

Trains made of marzipan glide so fast,
Delivering giggles that forever last.
Jellybean stars light up the night,
While cheerful cupcakes take flight.

Toffee trolls with their jiggly charm,
Creating mischief with candy yarn.
Bouncy brownies leap with glee,
As the gumdrops toss carelessly.

Memories sweet like honey on toast,
In this land where silliness boasts.
With smiles and laughter all around,
In this funny world, joy's always found.

Dreamy Delights of Chilly Evenings

Peppermint sticks in my hot drink,
An elf starts to dance, makes me rethink.
Marshmallow snowflakes fall from the sky,
I laugh so hard, I think I might cry.

Frosty the snowman wearing a scarf,
Chasing a reindeer, oh what a laugh!
Sugar plums giggle in festive delight,
As snowmen throw snowballs all through the night.

Sweets of the Solstice Serenade

Gumdrops and laughter all blend with cheer,
As my cat steals a treat, oh dear, oh dear!
Lollipops dangling from every tree,
Elves in a conga line, happy and free.

Fudge flies by on a peppermint sleigh,
And candy canes sing as they dance and play.
Winking gingerbread wave hello,
In this jolly land where sweet dreams grow.

A Cookie's Journey Through Snowy Streets

A cookie named Chip took a snowy stroll,
On an adventure towards the bakery roll.
He met with a pie in a frosty coat,
Together they laughed, oh what a note!

Frosting so thick, it made them both trip,
Socks made of sprinkles went slipping and flip.
With friends all around and sweet treats galore,
Chip grinned wide, he couldn't ask for more.

Sprinkles of Joy in the Arctic Air

Sprinkles are dancing in frosty delight,
As snowflakes join in, it's quite a sight!
A marshmallow army rolls down the lane,
Waging a battle with sugar-sweet rain.

Fluffy penguins slide on candy ice,
Making giggles with every roll, so nice!
Fudge penguins gather, they shake their tails,
In this wonderland where laughter prevails.

Twists and Turns of Holiday Flavor

Twisted treats upon the shelf,
Grinning like a sneaky elf.
Colors bright, a clashing sight,
Who knew sweets could bring such light?

Lollipop sticks in a dance,
A sugary swirl, a frosted chance.
Peeking round, they laugh and play,
Hoping to brighten up our day.

Tasty troubles without a care,
Chasing dreams we all can share.
Gingerbread spies in the night,
Mischief runs till morning light.

Thumbs up for the frosty cheer,
Laughter echoes, spreading near.
Biting bites of pure delight,
Holiday giggles take their flight.

Swirls of Whimsy on the Table

Plates are piled, a sight to see,
Whirlwinds of joy, fun and glee.
Jellybeans jump, marshmallows sing,
Sticky fingers dance in spring.

Frosted cookies with silly grins,
Frosting laughter, where it begins.
Sipping cocoa with a twist,
Chilly nights can't be missed!

Gummy bears plotting their schemes,
Whispers float on winter's dreams.
Chocolate coins make mischief take,
With every bite, another wake.

Savoring flavors, a chaotic blend,
Each sweet treat is sure to send,
Us tumbling through a frosted tide,
With laughter as our joyful guide!

Sweets to Savor by the Fireside

By the fire, the stories flow,
Sugar sprinkles, warm aglow.
Chewy treats, a flickering beam,
Chasing away the cold night’s dream.

Nutty surprises in every bite,
Flavors mingle with pure delight.
Toasty hugs in every sip,
Spreading warmth, let’s take a dip!

Chocolate drizzles, smeared with glee,
Bringing joy like holiday tea.
Crackling laughter, a toast of cheer,
Silly tales that we hold dear.

Sweetened whispers 'neath the moon,
Crackers crunch in our festive tune.
Fireside laughs and a friendly tease,
Salted caramel brings us ease!

Clandestine Nibbles of Yuletide Joy

In the shadows do they creep,
Nibbling secrets while we sleep.
Cookies dashed and candies bare,
Mischief lingers in the air.

Chocolates peek from corners tight,
Snacking stealthily each night.
Giggling jellies hide and seek,
Silly mouths with sugar streaks.

Syrupy dreams drip down the walls,
Behind the doors, the laughter calls.
Fruitcake giggles in the fray,
Wishing us a sweeter day.

Under blankets, whispers rise,
Joyful grins and twinkly eyes.
Merry munchers of hidden glee,
A feast of laughter, wild and free!

Winter's Essence in a Sweet Embrace

Frosty air with treats in hand,
Laughter echoes through the land.
A sleigh ride made of licorice,
In frosted fields, we find our bliss.

Chubby cheeks with sticky smiles,
Over hills, we race for miles.
Snowflakes twirl like sugar sprinkles,
Joyful jests, our laughter twinkles.

Gingerbread men with candy hats,
Sledding down on sugar mats.
A sprinkle here, a giggle there,
With every bite, we shed our care.

In whimsical worlds, we spin and sway,
With every treat, we dance and play.
A tub of fudge, the silly way,
Makes winter nights feel like ballet.

Spectacular Sweets of the Season

Chocolate rivers flow with glee,
Sugar clouds embrace the spree.
Marzipan with silly faces,
In our hearts, pure joy embraces.

Noses cold, but hearts are warm,
Chasing visions of sweet charm.
Fudge is melting, oh my me!
Can't resist this jubilee.

Wobbly tummies, laughter spills,
While we munch on sugary thrills.
A candy fight? Oh, what a blast!
Frosty fun that’s built to last.

With every giggle, we will cheer,
For every treat that brings us near.
In this season, we truly bloom,
A chorus sung in sugar's room.

Cheerful Delights Wrapped in Ribbons

Ribbons twirl on every treat,
Joyful giggles fill the street.
A frosty bite brings on the cheer,
With every laugh, we spread good cheer.

Bubble baths of syrupy fun,
Lollipops glimmer in the sun.
A treasure hunt for odd delights,
Tasting giggles on frosty nights.

Pinecones dipped in sweetened glaze,
Silly socks in bright arrays.
Underneath the twinkling lights,
We find our joy in winter nights.

With marshmallows in every bowl,
We play and share our simple goals.
A season filled with funny sights,
As laughter dances through the nights.

Gleaming Ornaments and Sugary Cravings

Glistening bulbs in colors bright,
Sweets come out to join the night.
A tree adorned with jelly beans,
As we plot our sugar dreams.

Whipped cream mountains tower high,
With every scoop, we touch the sky.
Cookies crunch, and giggles soar,
In the wonder, we explore.

Surprises hide in every nook,
Giggling kids and storybooks.
A candy trail, we follow fast,
In this sweet world, we're unsurpassed.

Gleaming joy in every bite,
In our hearts, the season's light.
With every moment, laughs will grow,
In a sugary wind's gentle blow.

Starry Nights and Sugar Cravings

Under twinkling lights above,
We hunt for sweetness in a cove.
With each bite, a giggle bursts,
Our silly cravings, they just thirst.

Lollipop sticks in Santa's sack,
The peppermint mouse starts to crack.
As we dance with joy and cheer,
The wild sugar rush draws us near.

Marshmallow clouds in cocoa seas,
We drift along with sticky knees.
In this land of frosty fun,
Who needs sleep? The night's begun!

Gingerbread men with grins so wide,
Jump around on a frosted ride.
Sugary dreams fill the night air,
While chasing after sweet despair.

Sugarplum Fancies in the Air

Bouncing balls of frosting delight,
As sugarplums take off in flight.
The cocoa river flows so free,
While caramels dance in glee.

Sprinkles fall like cheerful rain,
Every taste is a sweet refrain.
Chocolate ducks chase jellybeans,
In this land of giggles and dreams.

Dangling licorice from the tree,
Teasing squirrels play hide and seek.
Whipped cream clouds drift overhead,
As candy thoughts spin in our heads.

Sugar spritz and whipped fluff cheers,
Wibbly wobbly, let's shift gears.
With jelly joy and fizzy thrills,
We unwrap laughter, hugs, and chills.

Dreams Unwrapped on Merry Eve

Crinkly packages lie about,
The candy stash, we twist and shout.
A candy explosion is our fate,
Let's unwrap giggles, don't be late!

Chocolates dance on mistletoe,
With every bounce, the laughter grows.
Toffee whispers soft and sweet,
While gummy bear pirates claim their seat.

Fruity flavors break the night,
As marshmallow snowflakes soar in flight.
Glitter trails from cookie pies,
With giggles bubbling from our eyes.

We ride on a candy cane sleigh,
Hopping through a sugary display.
In this wild candy-structured dream,
We laugh and tumble, how extreme!

Bright Hues of Sweets and Cheer

Rainbow swirls and bright confetti,
The holiday cheer is oh so ready.
Candy flowers bloom on the table,
In this silly feast, we’re all stable.

With gumdrops stacked like little towers,
We giggle for hours and hours.
Marzipan figures join the spree,
In this zany world, we feel so free.

Fizzy drinks with bursts of zest,
Who knew sweets could be such a fest?
A pie made of laughter, crust of cheer,
Let's take a bite, the party’s here!

In this bubble of sugar and fun,
Every moment is a sweet run.
The night rolls on with joyous screams,
In our wild land of sugary dreams.

Whirls of Delight on a Frosty Eve

Twinkling lights dance in the snow,
Nose turns red, cheeks aglow.
Socks are hung with glee and flair,
Who knows what surprises are hiding there?

Nibbled crumbs lead to the door,
Squeaky toys, we can't ignore!
Giggles rise like the cold wind's cheer,
Watch out for the sneaky deer!

Jingle bells sound from the roof,
We half-believed, oh what a goof!
Eggnog spills on the living room floor,
Laughter bubbles – come for more!

Snowflakes whirl in a frosty game,
Mittens lost, but who's to blame?
Heartfelt wishes float in the air,
Frosty poems lettered with care.

Tempting Tidings of Yuletide Bliss

Gingerbread men run for their lives,
Caught in a chase where mischief thrives.
Tinsel tangled in a high tree,
Grandma's knitting brings back glee.

Sugar plums bounce on the floor,
While puppies chew on the neighbor's door.
Chocolates hidden by sneaky hands,
Who knew cocoa made such plans?

Bells ring louder as kids take flight,
Sleds crash into a snowball fight.
Frosted windows frame the show,
And frosty mischief steals the glow!

Friends and family share a toast,
With silly hats, we play the host.
Laughter echoes, bright and clear,
As joy spills over with holiday cheer.

Holiday Hues and Sweeten'd Dreams

Colors splash in a joyful sweep,
Tracked in snow, not one winced peep.
Winking lights on a bright display,
Puppies bark in their playful sway.

Marshmallow clouds fill the night sky,
Join the dance, don't be shy!
Pies on windowsills, they twirl,
Careful now, you might give a whirl!

Giggles sprout from every nook,
Whiskers twitch by a storybook.
Socks are mismatched, oh what a sight,
But warmth and love fill the night!

Ribbons fly as we unwrap,
Happy chaos, a festive trap.
In sweetened dreams, we take a flight,
Through silly whispers of pure delight.

Glistening Frost and Flavorful Fantasies

Icicles spark like diamonds bright,
Maybe eat one? That’ll be a fright!
Snowmen waddle, their hats a bit loose,
They giggle and wiggle, what’s the excuse?

A cookie jar that’s deemed a trap,
Bakers whistle, hear that clap!
Flour fights in the kitchen's charm,
Sifting giggles, it’s all part of the charm!

Holiday tunes on loop, oh dear,
Silly dances bring us near.
With every shake of our merry tails,
We dive into the whimsical tales!

Frosty wind whispers tunes aglow,
Chasing laughter as we go.
In this moment, we bravely dream,
Of all the fun, or so it seems!

Harvesting Happiness in Gaily Wrapped Sweets

A jolly jar filled with gleaming treats,
Peculiar flavors that twist and greet.
Lollipop laughs and gumdrop cheer,
Sweet surprises for all who come near.

Giggling elves with sugar on their cheeks,
Nibbles and giggles for merry techniques.
Each crinkly wrapper tells a goofy tale,
As sticky fingers from munching prevail.

Frosted smiles in a sugary rush,
Mirthful munching, a delightful hush.
Beneath a tree that’s twinkling bright,
The laughter echoes through the chilly night.

With every bite, a chuckle's near,
An avalanche of sweets, we'll share some cheer!
These treats unite us in silly delight,
Harvesting happiness from morning till night.

Brightly Colored Wishes Cascading Down

In the frosty air, colors brighten the lane,
Marshmallow clouds fluff out the mundane.
With rippling ribbons of vibrant hue,
Wishes sprinkle like confetti, too!

Giggles scatter like windswept flakes,
Each one demanding a taste, for goodness' sakes!
A whirlwind of sweetness, bizarre and fun,
Mixing up flavors 'til the day is done.

Postcards of laughter wrapped in glee,
Each one a treasure, as wild as can be.
Chuckles ignite like twinkling lights,
As we share stories on these wintry nights.

Gumball dreams rolled into a ball,
As we tumble and frolic, embracing it all.
With brightly colored wishes a-cometh around,
Gathering joy in the night's spinning sound.

Magical Morsels in the Silent Night

In the deep of the night, magic grabs hold,
Morsels of wonder, stories retold.
Fudgey surprises spark giggling delight,
In a quiet chaos, the sweets take flight.

Tasty bites shine like stars up above,
Each one whispers warmth, kindness, and love.
The gingerbread men dance on the floor,
With sugary swag, and so much in store.

With every sweet nibble, laughter climbs high,
Bantering cookies, oh my! Oh my!
Sugary secrets in whimsical bites,
Cheering our spirits through chilly nights.

Let’s raise a toast with hot cocoa in hand,
As dreams swirl around like a merry band.
In the night's gentle hug, we find our refrain,
Magical morsels that tickle the brain.

Frosty Breezes and Irresistible Treasures

Frosty gusts carry sweet-scented dreams,
Whispers of mischief, and comic extremes.
With hasty steps, we dance in delight,
Chasing the giggles that soar through the night.

A parade of goodies all wrapped up tight,
Each one a trinket of laughter and light.
Chocolate might tumble, while jellies coo,
In the joyful pandemonium, all flavors accrue.

As we frolic about, flavors bounce and collide,
Tickling our fancy with every great stride.
These treasures hold stories that sparkle and shine,
In the playful wind’s embrace, all is divine.

So let's fill our pockets with whimsical fun,
And embrace the cheer that is never outrun.
Frosty breezes blow through laughs, oh so bold,
With irresistible treasures waiting to be told.

Heavenly Delights on Glimmering Nights

On rooftops high, we peek and stare,
With fluffy hats and freezing air.
Sugar plums dance and twirl with glee,
While snowflakes giggle like kids at a spree.

The sleds go fast, the laughter loud,
As hot cocoa warms the freezing crowd.
Lollipop trees sway in delight,
Under the moon's shiny, silvery light.

Elves on swings take goofy leaps,
As jolly folks forget their heaps.
With marshmallow clouds drifting near,
We toast to joys only found right here.

Joyful chuckles spill and blend,
In festive fun that'll never end.
We nibble treats and share our cheer,
With silly grins that last all year.

Sweet Spices and Whirlwinds of Happiness

Cinnamon scents fill up the air,
While giggles wrap 'round without a care.
Frosted windows hide all the mess,
As puppets perform in their finest dress.

Riding the whirlwind of sugary bliss,
Each bite's a dance, a joyful kiss.
Fudge drips down with a comic flair,
Leaving everyone to twist and share.

Marzipan mountains stack so high,
As dessert dreams flutter and fly.
The laughter echoes around the room,
While gingerbread houses start to boom.

Sprinkles tumble and take a bow,
As sweethearts giggle—not knowing how.
In a whirlwind of giggles and treats,
We flip through joy in swirly feats.

Yule's Best on Every Plate

Pudding plops with a jolly grin,
While revelers cheer and joy begins.
Mashed potatoes simply whirl and spin,
And laughter bursts forth like a violin.

Turkey wobbles like it knows a joke,
As family members dance and poke.
With pies that bounce and cookies that sing,
The table's a stage for this festive fling.

Silly hats and wines that fizz,
We toast to bliss with a raucous whizz.
The best of meals on every plate,
Bring out the fun, there's no time to wait!

In a world of smiles and joyous cheer,
Every bite's filled with holiday gear.
With puns and giggles we share our fate,
In a feast that’s sure to resonate.

Bows and Bonbons under the Stars

Under twinkling lights, we find our way,
With bows that wiggle and sweets that play.
The stars above giggle with delight,
As we munch on dreams all through the night.

Bonbons bouncing in laughter's embrace,
While silly songs quicken the pace.
We twirl around in the frosty chill,
While sugar-kissed giggles give us a thrill.

Ornaments jingle, a charming sound,
As we ride the waves of joy all around.
With every twirl underneath the moon,
We burst into laughter in a festive tune.

The night wraps us up in a cozy glow,
Where giggles and sweet treats endlessly flow.
With bows and bonbons, we sing with glee,
On a sparkling night, just you and me.

Sweet Moments of Holidazzle

In a forest made of gumdrops bright,
Elves dance under twinkling light.
Marshmallow bunnies hop with glee,
While Santa sips from his fizzy tea.

Frosty giggles, a snowman rolls,
Tinsel tickles, and laughter strolls.
Sugar sprinkles rain from above,
It's a chaotic, sweet-filled love.

Lollipops spin like merry stars,
Jingle bells slide down candy bars.
A hiccup or two from sipping cheer,
As buddies yell, “Let’s eat some weird!”

With every crunch and every bite,
The night turns silly, pure delight.
Holidazzle, oh what a spree,
In sugar-coated fantasy!

Winter's Treats and Timeless Carols

Icicles drip like sugary streams,
Frosty windows hide giggling screams.
Statues made of peppermint stripes,
Making faces, oh, how they hype!

Snowflake ballet on sugary toes,
Plum puddings prance in goofy rows.
A chorus of laughing, sweet-faced friends,
With frosting and cheer that never ends.

Jingle socks thrown over the chair,
Muffins singing without a care.
As spice twirls round in spiraled glint,
The snowmen giggle—who needs a hint?

With jingles and rumbles of joyful cheer,
We celebrate in winter's sphere.
Timeless laughter, a jolly spree,
With recipes spilling laughter, oh me!

Enchanted Sweets of December's Glow

Chocolate rivers flow bright and bold,
As reindeer swoosh, making tales told.
Cookies dance in frosted delight,
Tickling elves as they twirl all night.

Candy castles made of sticky bliss,
One slip and you might go amiss!
But who cares when gumdrops flow?
Every giggle is a star in tow.

Pudding puddles—oops, what a mess!
Jolly friends in sweetened dress.
Whipped cream clouds in the frosty air,
Why take caution? Who wouldn't dare?

With laughter echoing through the trees,
Each moment tastes like honeybees.
December's glow, an enchanted spree,
Filled with sweetness and pure glee!

Sugar’s Embrace in a Starry Night

Under a sky of crushed candy glow,
A family gathers, popcorn in tow.
Sprinkled wishes float with the stars,
As puppies devour old chocolate bars.

Marzipan moons dance on the ground,
While giggling youngsters twirl all around.
Ticklish tastes of chewy delight,
A frosty venture 'til the morning light.

Muffin monsters stumble and trip,
Chasing that last sweet, taking a sip.
A sprinkle fight breaks out, oh dear,
Sugar explosions, but no one fears!

With hearts so full, through the chilly breeze,
We toast to laughter and sugary flurries.
A starry night, a delightful chase,
Where every sweet brings a smiling face!

Joyful Nibbles on a Starry Night

In the pantry, snacks take flight,
Marshmallows bounce with pure delight,
Chocolates giggle in their wrappers,
As kids munch on with silly snappers.

Gumdrops dance around the place,
While lollipops put on a race,
Winking at the joyful glee,
Sweet treats laughing endlessly.

Baking pies with silly hats,
Who knew dough could play like that?
Pudding cups start to sing,
When sugar high becomes the king!

Crisp cookies jive on a plate,
Yummy whispers escalate,
With every bite, a wacky cheer,
Nibbles spread the festive cheer!

Sweetness Lingers in the Air

In the kitchen, chaos reigns,
Flour flies like softest rains,
Icing twirls with a funny sound,
As holiday giggles swirl around.

Fruit cakes wobble with grim glee,
While gingerbread men claim to flee,
Chewy caramel tries to stroll,
Sticky mischief takes its toll.

Cupcakes wear their fanciest hats,
Spreading joy like silly spats,
Sprinkles twinkle in the night,
As goodies shine with delight.

Brownies wiggle on their stance,
While truffles do a little dance,
Lollies whisper jokes so sweet,
Creating laughter in the heat!

Shimmering Dreams of Frosty Nights

Outside the window, snowflakes dart,
While licorice trees make a start,
Jelly beans on frosted grass,
Spreading giggles as they pass.

Sugar plums in winter's clutch,
Huddle 'round for a sweetness touch,
Marzipan winks from the shelf,
Subtle dreams of tasty wealth.

Whipped cream clouds float on by,
Squeaky chairs let out a sigh,
Cocoa spills with giggles galore,
As laughter echoes through each door.

Cherries play hopscotch on the beams,
While the pudding sings sugary dreams,
With every bite, the fun resumes,
In a dance of sweetened blooms.

Glorious Treats of Yuletide Splendor

Pudding pops wear happy faces,
While candy apples flaunt their laces,
Every nibble tells a tale,
In this whimsical festive gale.

Muffins giggle in their tins,
As the laughter and joy begins,
Taffy has its own parade,
Candy joy will never fade.

Donuts roll on plates of cheer,
Happily munching, never fear,
Frosting glistens, a sugary treat,
As treats form a dazzling fleet.

With each bite, sweet memories grow,
In this land where laughter flows,
A holiday feast where smiles linger,
With every calorie, a joyful singer!

Dashing Through Sweets of Winter's Tail

Oh, look at that giant gumdrop snowman,
He's losing his hat, oh what a plan!
Sugarplum fairies are dancing in glee,
While the toffee trees sway, come join the spree!

Frosted pretzels hang from the eaves,
Children giggle under sugary leaves.
Marshmallow hills are rolling with cheer,
Tickling our noses, oh winter, oh dear!

Lollipop lanterns light up the night,
With caramel stars shining oh so bright.
Chasing the giggles through drifts of delight,
A world made of sweetness, everything's right!

Can you imagine a candy-inspired sleigh?
With jellybean reindeer leading the way.
We dash through the treats, hearts filled with fun,
Laughing and feasting till the day is done!

Lush Landscapes of Frosted Goodies

Welcome to the land of frosted delights,
Where chocolate rivers flow past sugary heights.
Here gingerbread houses whisper and sing,
And pudding ponds are the freshest of bling!

The icicles shimmer like licorice sticks,
While peppermint penguins perform silly tricks.
Fizzy pop shrubs drape in snowflake attire,
As we feast on the whims of a sugary choir!

Licorice vines tangle in candy cane curls,
While marshmallow clouds drift and twirl.
Squirrels in frocks nibble on cream,
In this jolly land, life’s a sweet dream!

Hilarity bursts with every sweet bite,
Making even sour patches feel just right!
Join in the laughter, don't be shy,
Here in the frosted sky, candies fly high!

Melodies of Mirth and Flavorful Cheer

Dances of jellybeans twirl in the breeze,
As gaggles of gumdrops hum jolly tunes with ease.
Candy flutes play sugar-sweet rhymes,
Bringing levity, laughter, and fun times!

Chocolate bunnies hop on licorice trails,
While the cotton candy wind tells juicy tales.
Ribbons of caramel weave through the scene,
As the candy chorus bursts forth with glee!

Sing, little treats, in this sugary spree,
With frosty cupcakes as our party marquee.
Tickly sprinkles tickle our playful hearts,
Creating sweet memories, our laughter imparts!

Lemon drops drip from the sun's golden ray,
While candy wrappers dance, twirling away.
Join in as we sway and sway through the night,
In this mirth-filled symphony of pure delight!

Sparkling Sweets in a Winter Glade

In a glade brimming with frosted delight,
Where gumdrop towers rise to new heights.
Frosty cupcakes gleam like stars in the sky,
While the wand of a wink inspires each sigh.

A snowman with jellybeans buttons to cheer,
Chortles from elves ring throughout the year.
The cocoa stream bubbles, inviting a sip,
Oh, the laughter and swirls on this whimsical trip!

Gummy bears guide us where laughter erupts,
Through fields full of sweets, where joy is abruptly.
Laughter erupts as we tumble and slide,
In this dreamy retreat, let glee be our guide!

So gather your friends, your laughter, your cheer,
In these sparkling sweets, bring all of you near.
Unwrap the magic, let merriment stay,
In the glade full of wonder, let's play, play, play!

Enchanted Flavors of the Festive Season

In the land of frosty treats,
Elves dance to the jingle beats.
Licorice lollipops swirl around,
Marshmallow clouds that bounce and bound.

Gumdrops giggle in the night,
Sugar sprinkles, oh what a sight!
Chocolate rivers flow with glee,
Taste the magic, come and see.

Fudge fountains, creamy peaks,
Spicy gingerbread that speaks.
Jolly jellybeans, bright and bold,
Stories of joy and laughter told.

So grab a taste that's oh so fun,
In this flavor-packed holiday run!
With every nibble, laughter grows,
In this world of sweetened woes.

Memories Sweetened with Laughter

Laughter bubbles like hot cocoa,
With marshmallows dancing, oh what a show!
Each chuckle tastes like peppermint cheer,
Reminding us to hold joy near.

Giggling gumdrops in a bowl,
Wiggling wrappings ready to roll.
Every giggle, a memory made,
In this candy-coated escapade.

Nostalgia sprinkled all around,
With sugar highs, we're joyfully bound.
Toffee whispers tales of old,
With laughter's warmth, we're never cold.

So let's munch on delight and glee,
Sharing laughter like candy!
With every bite and happy cheer,
Our sweetest memories draw near.

Delicious Doubles in a Winter Wonderland

Twinkling lights on licorice trees,
Sipping cocoa, feeling the breeze.
Chocolate sleighs go whoosh and zoom,
While sugarplum fairies decorate the room.

Waffles stacked with syrupy dreams,
They giggle and wobble, bursting at seams.
Frosted cupcakes, a whimsical sight,
With sprinkles that sparkle under moonlight.

Marzipan penguins sliding by,
Giggling gingerbread, oh me, oh my!
With each joyful bite a new surprise,
In this winter wonderland, laughter flies.

So come and taste the funny delight,
In this frozen feast, we'll stay up all night!
As flavors warm our chilled souls near,
In doubles of joy, there's nothing to fear!

Whimsical Delights Beneath the Snow

Frosty flakes are powdered sweet,
Where jellybeans and bunnies meet.
Candy canes like snowflakes swirl,
In a giggling, twirling, candy whirl.

Charmed by chocolate, we prance and play,
In a winter wonder, come join the fray!
With every sprinkle of sugar and cheer,
The fun tastes better when friends are near.

Sugar-snapped giggles in the cold,
Whimsical wonders, brave and bold.
Frosty figures in a sugary dream,
With laughter and love, we’re a perfect team.

So let’s snicker beneath the snow,
Sharing sweet tales as our joy will grow!
Beneath the snowy, magical light,
These whimsical delights keep our hearts bright.

Gingerbread Lullabies of Frosty Mornings

In a house made of sweets, how could I snore?
Sugarplum fairies dance, shouting encore!
Gumdrops are giggling, they're stuck on the wall,
Whipped cream clouds giggle, and ice cream might fall.

Frosty the snowman, he’s lost his three buttons,
Chased by a squirrel, they’re playing for gluttons.
Chocolate chip cookies have started to fight,
Who baked the best batch? It's a cookie delight!

Marshmallow snowflakes are falling so soft,
Tickling my nose as they drift from aloft.
Underneath twinkling lights, bright as a star,
I dream of a world made sweet with bizarre.

Lollipops twirl like a circus parade,
Candy-coated laughter that never will fade.
A peppermint chorus sings loud from the tree,
At dawn, all the sweets shout, 'Come play with me!'

Joyful Moments Wrapped in Ribbon

Presents piled high, like a mountain of cheer,
Wrapping paper fights bust out every year.
Ribbons are tangled, oh what a big mess,
Giggling child wrestles, both happy and stressed.

Frosted cupcakes play hide and seek on a plate,
One took a dive, and it's now on a date!
While jellybeans argue on who's got the best,
A cherry on top, but they're still quite pressed.

Giggles erupt from a hidden stash,
As ginger snaps try for a speedy dash.
Bouncing from shelves with marshmallows in tow,
They've taken a trip to the land of the glow!

With sprinkles like stars flying high in the night,
The candy rulers bicker, who's wrong and who's right?
In a whirlwind of wonder, the holidays spin,
In a laughter-filled frenzy, the fun just begins!

Euphoria in Every Sugar Flake

Frosty air tickles as I breathe in deep,
Sugar snow falling, it’s beauty I keep.
Each flake a giggle, each drift a sweet cheer,
Skipping through wonder, the season is here.

Candy-coated laughter spills out from the cup,
Hot cocoa swimming, saying 'Drink me up!'
Tiny marshmallows staging a grand play,
In a whimsical tale that won’t fade away.

Gingerbread folk are assembling a crew,
Plotting a heist for the frosting they knew.
Chasing away crumbs with their sprightly feet,
A world made of sugar, can’t be beat!

In a bubble of fun where children can twirl,
Every sweet whisper, their hearts start to whirl.
Dancing through days made of colorful sighs,
In every sugar flake, a mystery lies!

Celestial Confections and Mirthful Skies

Under the starlight, the candies take flight,
Sprinkling joy in the magical night.
Starbursts collide in a raspberry whirl,
With a twist of the tongue, my taste buds unfurl.

Giggling gummies lounge on velvet blue clouds,
Jellybean dreams whisper sweet, playful shrouds.
Popcorn kernels burp, what a raucous surprise,
Rocketing laughter erupts from their eyes.

With icing rivers flowing under the moon,
Sugar plums are flirting, they dance to the tune.
Marzipan mountains rise swift from the ground,
Sprinkling cheer in the air all around.

In this land of sweets, where the absurd feels right,
Laughter and joy twinkle, oh what a delight!
From candies to giggles that light up the skies,
Each moment together, a wonderful prize!

Sugar Stripes and Frosted Nights

Beneath the snowflakes, all aglow,
A peppermint army puts on a show.
They march and wiggle with sticky grace,
As gumdrop guards keep watch in place.

The hot cocoa’s bubbling, giggles in air,
Chasing gingerbread men, with flair to spare.
Frosty’s got moves, he’s busting a rhyme,
Cocoa beans dance, feeling so sublime.

Marshmallows leap like they've lost their heads,
In this world of sweets, where mischief spreads.
Lollipops twirl, causing giggles galore,
Sugar-filled chaos, we all crave more!

Twinkling above, the stars start to cheer,
As candy canes hang, oh so near.
In this frosted wonder, we'll laugh and play,
A sweet little night, all in disarray.

Twinkling Delights of Winter's Embrace

In the still of the night, a choir of cats,
Wearing tiny hats and having chitchats.
Jingle bells jingle, they meow in tune,
Under a sky that's lit up like noon.

A bubblegum snowman, a sight so rare,
With a nose made of jellybeans, sweet as air.
He tells silly jokes, makes laughter arise,
In a world built of sweets, what a surprise!

Fudge falls like rain, oh what a delight,
As children run wild in the pale moonlight.
They scoop up the treats, putting smiles on faces,
In this sugary haven, where joy interlaces.

With sprinkles of laughter, love fills the night,
As the stars twinkle down, so warm and bright.
We embrace the madness, the delightful cheer,
In this frosty wonderland, we hold so dear.

Whispers of a Sweet Yuletide

The elves are crafting with glue and cheer,
Building wild toys that pop up each year.
Their giggles echo, mischievous tone,
As frosted marshmallows climb on a cone.

Something's amiss, the fruitcake's on fire,
A twinkling dessert that we all admire.
Its sugary scent fills the chilly air,
But no one dares touch, it’s a bold affair!

With candy corn trees that sway in the breeze,
And sugarplum fairies dancing with ease.
They sprinkle the air with sweet, silly dreams,
In a land where nothing is quite as it seems.

Sassy snowflakes, like comedians bold,
Telling sweet stories, forever retold.
With laughter and joy, our spirits take flight,
In this whimsical world, everything’s right.

Peppermint Wishes on Starry Slopes

The sledders zoom down with peppermint grins,
Steering with laughter as every one spins.
In this wintry wonder, giggles collide,
With sprinkles of joy on this frosty ride.

Marzipan mountains are ready to climb,
With the thrill of the frost and the jingle of time.
Everyone’s shouting, 'Let's hop on this train!'
As we hurtle down slopes, dodging snowball rain!

In this merry chaos, a snowball fight breaks,
With giggles and whoops, and some candy quake.
The reindeer are watching, with eyes open wide,
As we whirl in a dance, on this sweet, frosted slide.

With dreams in our hearts and joy in our soul,
We ride on the laughter as the night takes its toll.
In a frosted delight, with wishes all around,
There's magic in winter, that’s joyfully found.

Whimsical Treats Beneath the Tree

Beneath the tree, what do I see?
A giant cookie, staring back at me!
It winks, then smiles, says, "Take a bite!"
I nod, I giggle, what a silly sight!

A marshmallow snowman, oh so round,
With jellybean buttons all around.
He tells me jokes, quite absurd and sweet,
We laugh until we tumble from our seat.

The tinsel shines like frosty hair,
As fruitcake jokes float through the air.
I can’t resist this tasty show,
A peppermint parade; let's go, let’s go!

So here we dance, in treat-filled glee,
In a world so rich, delicious, and free.
With giggles and sweets, we’ll rule the night,
Beneath the tree, life feels just right!

Frosted Memories from Yesteryears

In a house adorned with shiny treats,
I find old recipes, what a feast!
Frosted laughs from times gone by,
With sugar highs that make me fly.

Grandma’s fudge, a wobbly mess,
A soft, gooey blob I must confess.
Yet every bite's a taste of love,
Like sweet hugs from above.

My childhood friends, they gather round,
With sticky fingers, joy abounds.
We reminisce, we crumble cake,
All while dodging an icing quake.

With glasses raised and sticky cheers,
We toast to sweets from bygone years.
In every nibble, a story stays,
Frosted memories form our days!

Lollipop Luminescence in December

In December's chill, a taste so bright,
Lollipops glow like stars at night.
Flavors dance on a merry tongue,
Each swirl a song that's just begun.

A cherry pop spins with a laugh,
It teases me, "Come on, take a half!"
With cotton candy clouds in the air,
My sweet tooth's calling, it's hardly fair.

Gumdrop trails lead the way to fun,
As licorice whips outshine the sun.
I skip and hop, my heart's a drum,
In this sugary world, how can I succumb?

December nights filled with bright delight,
With every lick, my worries take flight.
All is merry, all is sweet,
In this lollipop world, my joy's complete!

Peppermint Swirls and Cocoa Wishes

With swirling hues of green and white,
I sip my cocoa, oh what a sight!
Marshmallows float like dreams in a cup,
While candy bits dance, won't give up.

Each wish I pour into the steam,
Floats up like bubbles, chasing a dream.
A sprinkle of laughter, a dash of cheer,
In this mug of magic, I hold dear.

With every sip, a giggle spills,
As peppermint giggles give me thrills.
The spry little elves join by the fire,
As cocoa wish tales lift higher and higher.

So here’s to the sips and swirls we find,
In frosty nights, with hearts entwined.
Let laughter bubble, let joy be bold,
In this candy wonderland, adventures unfold!

Whimsical Wonders of a Frosty Wonderland

In a land where snowflakes play,
Little elves dance and sway.
Frosty hats atop their heads,
Cocoa rivers, marshmallow beds.

Giggling snowmen, oh what a sight,
Sledding down hills until the night.
With peppermint sticks, they twirl around,
In this frosty fun, joy is found.

Sugar plums float in the air,
Lollipop trees growing with flair.
Twinkling stars with smiles so wide,
In this whimsical ride, we glide.

Bouncing snowballs, funny and round,
Giggles and chuckles are all abound.
In a frosty wonderland's embrace,
Laughter and joy will leave a trace.

Traces of Happiness on Frosted Pines

Underneath the twinkling lights,
A squirrel plays with snowball fights.
Frosted pines stand tall and proud,
Whispers of laughter through the crowd.

Gingerbread men with spicy flair,
Hide in bushes, sneaky, rare.
Chasing each other in a race,
Winter giggles, a happy space.

Singing snowflakes, oh what a tune,
Dancing beneath the glowing moon.
With cheeks so rosy, smiles so bright,
Happiness fills the frosty night.

Icicles hang with silly grace,
A slip and a slid, what a face!
In the air, joy's sweet perfume,
Among frosted pines, fun will bloom.

Sugar Stripes and Winter Whispers

Sweet stripes swirl in busy hands,
Joyful giggles across the lands.
Colors burst in snowy light,
As laughter dances through the night.

Reindeer prance with jingle bells,
Splashing in joy, oh how it swells!
Underneath the frosted skies,
They share secrets, hide their sighs.

Mittens tossed in playful glee,
Snowflakes whirl like fish in spree.
A candy jar that smiles so wide,
Happiness in goodies, side by side.

Hop on snowboards, let's ride fast,
A whirlwind of fun, let's make it last!
Sugar stripes upon the trees,
Wrapped in laughter, carried on the breeze.

Festive Twists of Minty Delight

Sprinkles of mint in the chilly air,
Frosty creatures dance without a care.
Sweet surprises under silver skies,
Where giggles and joy become the prize.

A ginger cat in a woolen hat,
Pounces on snow with a graceful spat.
Chasing shadows with ups and downs,
Laughter ringing through snowy towns.

Drifting by in a flashy sleigh,
Swooping low, then rushing away.
Minty wishes wrapped in cheer,
Happiness thrumming, loud and clear.

Smiles and sparkles in every place,
Funny hats with a silly grace.
In this festive twist, we'll unite,
And share our giggles heartily tonight.

Milton Keynes UK
Ingram Content Group UK Ltd.
UKHW021350011224
451618UK00023B/234

9 789916 908808